Bear*ly*
Historical

MILNER CRAFT SERIES

bearly
HISTORICAL

Robynn-El

First published in 2000 by
Sally Milner Publishing Pty Ltd
PO Box 2104
Bowral NSW 2576
AUSTRALIA

© Robynn-El 2000

Design by Ken Gilroy
Editing by Lyneve Rappell
Photography by Andrew Elton

Printed in Hong Kong

*National Library of Australia
Cataloguing-in-Publication data:*

El, Robynn.
Bearly historical.

ISBN 1 86351 247 0

Cross-stitch. I. Title. (Series:
Milner craft series).

746.443

Dedication

To Graeme John and Darrell
Alexander, with love.

Heartfelt dedication to my Dad,
Frank Cambourn (1927-1968) and
to Francis Roy Ross (1894-1980),
my Grandpa. Thank you both for
watching over me from Heaven and
for sending me Keith.

Grateful acknowledgement for their
expertise in giving my bears their
final wild touch goes to Evelyn and
Jack Hill of E. J. Hill Art Framing.

CONTENTS

DESIGNS

(or "Frankly, my dear, I don't give a darn!")

PREFACE

I find it amazing that in the short span of time between my book Magic and Mystery in Cross Stitch and this spicier one, that my life has so dramatically changed. When I look at these bear designs I can see exactly where I was and what was happening, almost like the unfolding of a personal timeline.

Hollywood movies (I am a disgracefully dedicated John Wayne fan) and romantic stories have always inspired me, as you can see in my design 'Bearzan & Jane'. Bearzan looks a bit concerned at the way Jane Bear is clinging to his semi-naked torso. In 'Cleobeartra', the slave dares not look at his wine-sipping queen, reclining resplendently in her see-through harem pants upon the chaise lounge. With 'Wild West Bears', I have depicted a reconciliation scene between a cowboy and an Indian. In 'Scarlett O'Beara' the heroine looks quite mesmerised by her hero. (I could never understand the way she spurned Rhett!) With 'Beareo & Juliet' I made her man climb a rose-coloured trellis just to get a glimpse of his beloved.

I salute the Renaissance artist Raphael with my version of 'Raphbears' which depicts angelic serenity and innocence. 'Blood Brothers' was inspired by the exquisitely seductive novels of Anne Rice. I have the Vampire/polar bear glancing hungrily upon the warmth of his mate Superbear/brown bear who in turn, looks understandably worried.

'The Beartles' design honours that pop group which gave my generation so much joy. Take note of the drummer's nose, the trendy suits and the telling hairstyles. When I look at 'Faery Bears', the design which initiated this book of historically stretched artworks, I can see my indecision, my bravery in stepping out of the proverbial comfort zone and the choices I made at the time which propelled me towards a brighter, happier and more positive future.

One of my ideas of success is to walk into a stranger's house and see one of my completed designs hanging on a wall. Therein lies the challenge to begin stitching now! If you would like to contact me with any comments regarding this book, you can do so through my publishers Ian Webster and Libby Renney of Sally Milner Publishing. I would love to hear from you. Enjoy my designs. I send you white light and happy thoughts.

Robyn-El

INTRODUCTION

Cross-stitch is a simple yet effective stitch formed by two diagonal bars which cross at the centre. Half the stitch is laid in one journey from left to right, then the top bar is stitched on the return to form the cross. Cross-stitch can be used as borders, outlines, or to fill in a whole area. An even stitch tension is ensured as all top threads lie in the same direction.

A coloured photograph, chart with symbols, colour key and a list of materials to complete the design is provided. Arrows on the graph indicate the centre lines so, if the graph is displayed over a double page, it can be photocopied and joined together via the overlap given.

Thread numbers for DMC stranded cotton only are given. However, due to the fact I have named each colour clearly, confident stitchers can easily transfer the DMC numbers into another range of threads available on the market.

For each design I have used Aida 14 cloth, an unprinted evenweave fabric especially made for cross-stitch. Aida 18 can be used as long as the reader is aware that the completed design will be smaller and any added embellishments (i.e. beads) will be a little more intricate to sew. I have given instructions for Aida 14 fabric packs as they are very economical (no leftover fabric) and the colour choice is really impressive. They are available through mail order outlets.

Each small square on the graph represents one cross-stitch. Each symbol on the chart represents the colour of cotton to use as indicated by the key. If you are a beginner, do not hesitate to swap a colour (of either the Aida cloth or stranded cotton) to make the design uniquely yours. Simply remember to practise all stitches first so you can produce them with ease and smooth, correct tension.

Level of difficulty

My designs are not aimed at a specific level of competence. You may be a beginner, an advanced stitcher or a creatively talented needleworker. Not everything in life needs to be ranked for enjoyment!

Each design uses the techniques of **cross-stitch**, $^1/_4$ and $^3/_4$ **cross-stitch** and **backstitch** with the addition of: **straight stitch** ('Beartles', 'Cleobeartra', 'Faery Bears'), overhand knots ('Faery Bears', 'Wild West Bears', 'Beareo & Juliet') and plaiting ('Wild West Bears').

Small **bugle beads** are sewn on 'Bearzan & Jane' and 'Scarlett O"Beara'. **Loose threads** for special effects are employed in 'Faery Bears' and 'Beareo & Juliet'. 'Cleobeartra' also uses two threads of different colours to create the see-through quality of her harem pants, which is simply stunning.

The extra patience and skill required to complete my designs is definitely worth the effort for the professional finish of your work.

MATERIALS

Aida 14 count in chosen colour, sold in fabric packs 30 cm x 45 cm (12" x 18") or by the metre with a width of 110 cm (43 $^1/_2$").

- Size 24 or 26 tapestry needle for evenweave fabrics.
- A pair of embroidery scissors.
- DMC stranded cotton in nominated colours (including metallic gold).
- A lap frame or scroll bars. I prefer a lap frame as it is small enough to travel with. I carry my chart in a plastic sleeve, which I place – along with the project on the lap frame – inside a pillowcase to keep them clean. Scroll bars are also popular as the fabric can be slid into the slot and the side bars attached without the need for lacing or stapling. Using either the lap frame or scroll bars allows you to stitch quickly, as you work with one hand on top of the fabric and one below it, with the weight of the piece resting against a table for support.

The following accessories are attractive for the serious cross-stitcher:

- Lo-Ran Line Magnifier, Magnetic Board (I use the 8" x 10") and Folding Stand. I place my chart on the magnetic board (attached by the given magnetic strips), which is held upright against the folding stand for easy viewing. The line magnifier is a transparent ruler with a red interior metallic strip which allows you to keep your exact place on the graph and see the row underneath which you have already completed. These products allow for hands-free convenience and pack flat for storage.
- Floss box to hold your threads.

Preparing fabric for stitching

Cut the Aida 14 to the size stated, or iron the creases out of the fabric pack Aida. Approximately 5 cm (2") of fabric allowance is included for framing purposes.

Overlock or oversew the edges of the Aida cloth to prevent fraying. Masking tape on the raw edges does the same job but can become stiff after a while.

To show the centre markings clearly, sew a thread in a darker colour than the Aida cloth horizontally and vertically. The centre is marked on all graphs in this book by tracking across the designs from the arrows on the edges of the design.

Mount the fabric into the embroidery frame or hoop as per the manufacturer's instructions, with the central stitch area at the centre.

It is preferable to begin stitching from the centre and work from the left to the right if you are right-handed. I tend to do either the left of a horizontally placed design, or the top of a vertically placed one, so that as I unroll the new area of fabric around the frame to complete the design, my work remains clean and dust-free within the completed part of the roll.

Hints for working cross-stitch

Use two strands of thread throughout the designs. To begin:

Method 1

Cut thread in lengths of 40 cm (15"). Separate the six strands into three strands of two. Thread your needle with two strands. Begin stitching by bringing the thread from underneath the work and holding about 1 cm (1/2") at the back. Work over this tail to secure it as you stitch a couple of squares. Never knot the thread.

Method 2

Cut double the length you desire, e.g. 60 cm (24") and double the cotton, threading the cut ends through the needle. To begin stitching, come up from the back of the fabric to make the first half of the cross (bottom left of the square) and plunge the needle through to the back again (top right of the same square), taking care to manoeuvre it through the loop made by the doubling, which catches it neatly at the back. No tail!

As each cross-stitch is made of two diagonal stitches, work one row making all left to right diagonal stitches in one colour, then return along that same row, crossing all stitches with right to left diagonals.

Always place the first stitches in the same direction, i.e. / / / / /, and place the second stitches so that they cross over \ \ \ \ \, making XXXXX.

Every so often, as you stitch, allow the needle to hang down to untangle the thread. This prevents the cotton from twisting in the fabric and looking thin and straggly.

To finish a colour, run the needle under approximately five stitches of the same colour at the back to secure, before snipping off the thread.

When using metallic thread, use a shorter length of thread and work these stitches last for a vivid impact.

Stitches

In my bear designs, I have used the full cross-stitch, $1/4$ and $3/4$ cross-stitch, backstitch and straight stitch. Overhand knots and bead embellishments are also explained below.

Full cross-stitch: For a row of cross-stitching, bring the needle up at the bottom left-hand corner (A), take

it down at B, bring it up at C, down at D and so on until you need to turn. Now bring the needle up at K, down at H, up at I, down at F and so

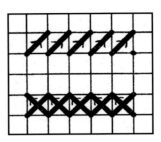

on, using the same holes as before.

For individual crosses or those on a slant, start at the lower left-hand corner of a square, bring the

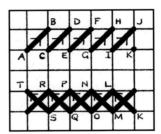

needle through to the front, then down at the upper right corner, up at the lower right and down at the upper left, which makes one perfect cross. Then bring the needle up again at the lower left-hand corner of the next square.

Quarter cross-stitch: You need to neatly utilise the centre of each square to complete three-quarter and quarter cross-stitches. Work the quarter cross-

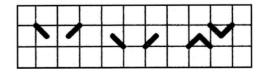

stitch into the centre of the square. Quarter stitches may begin from the left or right top corners and be worked down into the centre, or from the bottom left or right corners and up into the centre of the square. The rest of the square will either be filled up by a three-quarter cross-stitch in another colour, or left blank until you outline the whole area.

Three-quarter cross-stitch: These are useful stitches if you wish to avoid a sharp corner effect on a curve or for accentuating a pointed

shape. When working two colours in the same square, ensure the main colour forms the three-quarter cross-stitch and the subsidiary colour the quarter stitch.

Work the first half of the cross-stitch as per usual, but then take the second stitch down into the centre of the square, forming a quarter stitch.

Backstitch: I have used backstitch for detailing and outlining

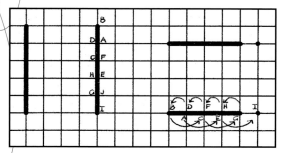

shapes. To work backstitch, bring the needle up at A, holding a 1 cm ($^1/_2$") tail at the back which you will secure

by stitching over, down at B, up at C, down at D, up at E, down at F and so on. Each stitch goes through the hole twice. Details worked in backstitch form a continuous line to outline or delineate certain areas.

Straight stitch: Bring the needle up at A, down at B, up at C, down at D, up at E, down at F, up at G, down at H and so on.

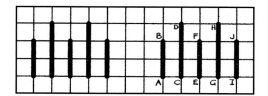

Overhand knots: Hold the end of the thread between your thumb and first finger. Wrap it around your middle finger, bring it up over the thumb-held section and under. Pull.

Sewing on beads: Using either normal sewing thread or your stranded cotton, attach each bugle bead as if you were sewing on a

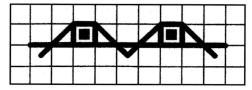

button with a shank. Secure properly at the back with a double stitch. Beads should be sewn on only when you have finished stitching the whole design.

Care of fabric

Before stitching, ensure your hands are clean so your fabric will not be soiled.

If you use an embroidery hoop, it is wise to remove your work from the hoop when you finish a stitching session to prevent creases and dirty marks. If you use a lap frame, sew the Aida cloth to the fabric tape strip with wool.

When in recess, cover your floor frame with a small cloth or put your lap frame in a pillowcase to keep the work from becoming dusty.

I check all my work closely with a magnifying glass when I have finished a project to ensure I have not missed a backstitched outline or delineated feature. Then I detach the fabric from the frame and wash it gently in a bucket of lukewarm water with a mild wool wash. A slight spray of pre-wash stain remover can help to remove any grubby marks. Dunk the fabric several times, leave it to soak for an hour and then flush it under cold running water until the water runs clear. Never wring the wet fabric, but roll it in a hand towel to dry, gently blocking by hand.

When dry, iron carefully on the wrong side, taking care to avoid any beads. Then, iron your work on the right side to place any loose hair or fringes properly, before framing.

Framing suggestions

I prefer to go to a professional framer as I believe that my time, energy and level of skill warrant the money spent to finish my work expertly. However, there are retail outlets where you can frame your work at a reasonable cost with the guidance of a specialist.

Choose a darker frame colour than the Aida cloth you used and try to highlight one of the main colours. A mounting board costs extra, but will set off your work exquisitely.

My bears do not have glass in their frames in this book for photographic reasons only. When the photographer had finished with them, I whipped them straight back to the professional framer who fitted each piece with clear glass, as I am very particular about not having my art damaged over time. Ask your framing expert for his or her opinion about the type of glass to use. The general rule is that clear glass is used unless the client specifically requests non-reflective glass. (Non-reflective glass is often chosen if the work is very dark, but unfortunately it takes away the clarity of both the colours and the details stitched.) There is no difference between the two types of glass in terms of preservation.

Never skimp on framing. You have put many hours of skill and love into your work, so show it off to advantage. Date and sign the back of the finished article too, as it may become a treasured family heirloom.

The **Bear**

D E S I G N S

FAERY BEARS

Faery
Bears

Robynn-El

FAERY BEARS

The finished design, measured at the exterior border pattern, is 27 cm high by 38 cm wide (10 $\frac{1}{2}$" x 15")

Fabric
A piece of 36 cm by 50 cm (14 $\frac{1}{2}$" x 20") pink Aida 14 cloth, slightly bigger than a fabric pack size to accommodate space around the border for framing.

Threads

Symbol	DMC thread	Colour
■	310	black
↓	335	deep medium pink
△	550	rich purple
Ø	600	crimson
N	702	light pea green
>	824	dark Aztec blue
*	898	mud brown
V	918	rich brown
\	972	gold
◿	976	pumpkin brown
▼	3755	pale sea blue

Techniques
* cross-stitch
* $\frac{1}{4}$ and $\frac{3}{4}$ cross-stitch
* backstitch
* overhand knots (bears' skirts)
* tacking (wands and stars on wings)

Instructions

- Unless otherwise stated, use two strands throughout the design, even for backstitch outlining.
- Backstitch 'Faery Bears' with 550 rich purple.
- Outline bodies of bears; paw details, noses, mouths, eyes, eyebrows and ears in 310 black.
- Outline the male bear's hat, vest and pocket delineation in 824 dark Aztec blue and his wings in 702 light pea green. His hatband is outlined in 3755 pale sea blue and his bow tie in 972 gold.
- Outline the pink wings of both female bears in 550 rich purple as well as the left bear's dress and the right bear's top.

Finishing

- Stars on the wings are tacked on in this order:
  A. Vertical stitch
  B. Horizontal stitch
  C. SW to NE cross bar, then
  D. SE to NW bar to match the direction of the other cross-stitches
- Outline the female bears' haloes and circlets on heads in 972 gold.
- The paired buttons on the middle bear's vest are made by cross-stitching the one square, backstitching it in the same 972 gold, then carrying the thread loosely to the corresponding button so it lies loosely on the vest like a fob watch chain. There are three pairs of these buttons.
- The haloes and stars on the wands are made from two strands of 972 gold with two strands of 600 crimson in the needle together to give a fuller effect.
- For the grass skirt effect on the female bears, I began by knotting at the back securely leaving a small tail, then I brought two threads of the cotton through to the appropriate dot (along the bottom row of the pink belt on the left bear and bottom row of the top of the right bear.) I knotted four overhand knots directly on the surface before cutting the thread between 1.5 to 2 cm ($^5/_8$" to $^6/_8$") in length. (I gave the left bear extra length on her skirt.) Working from left to right on the left bear, I used yellow, pink and green threads in that order. Working from left to right on the right bear, I used pink, green and yellow in that order all the way across.

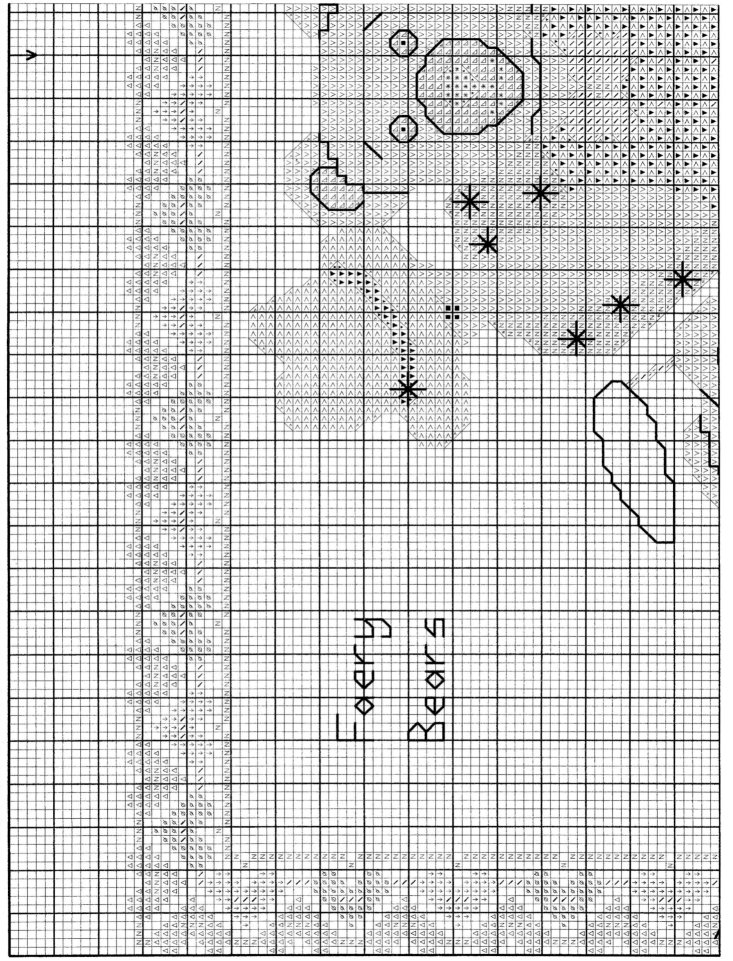

Enlarge 10%

Ⓐ

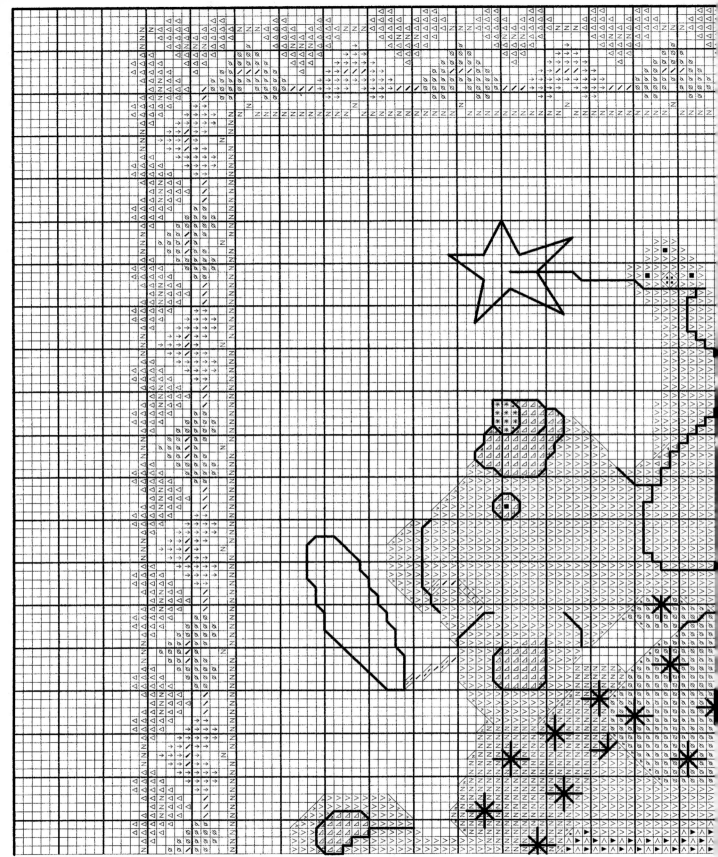

Enlarge 10%

B

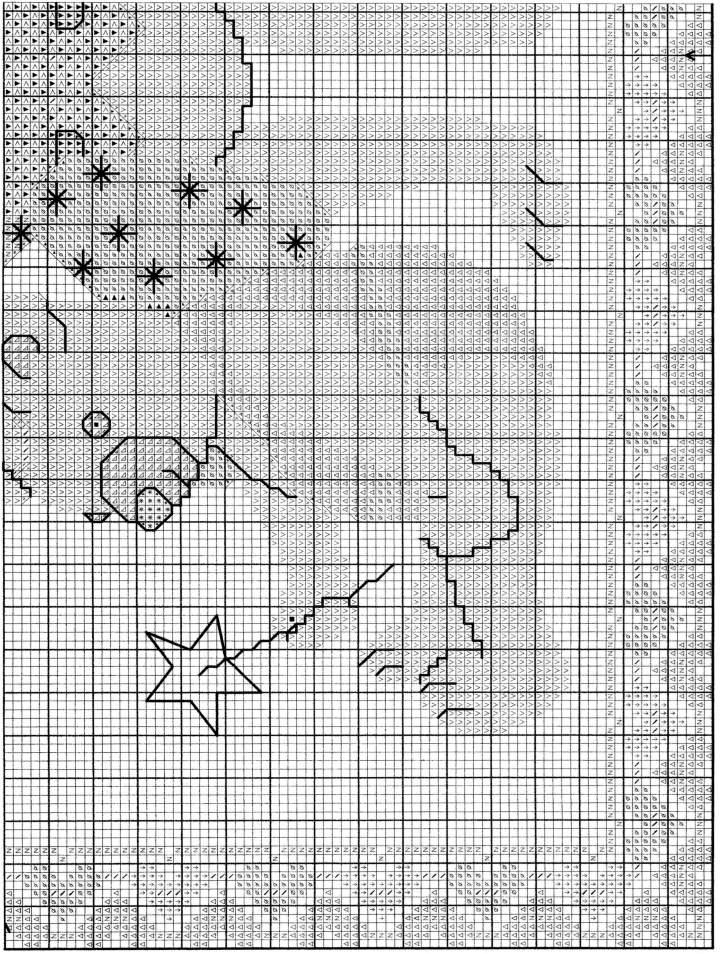

Enlarge 10%

Ⓒ

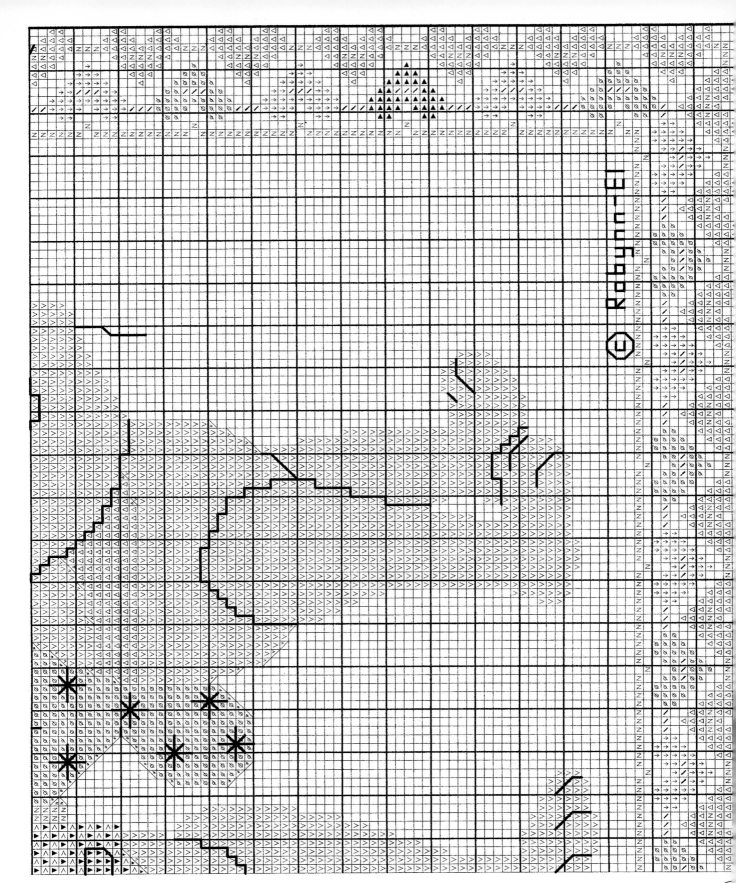

Enlarge 10%

WILD WEST BEARS

**The finished design measures 25 cm wide
by 31 cm high (9 $^3/_4$" x 12 $^1/_4$").**

Fabric
A 30 cm by 45 cm (12" x 18") piece of mid-green Aida 14
cloth (fabric pack size).

Threads

Symbol	DMC thread	Colour
▲	blanc	white
■	310	black
O	317	grey
↑	321	deep red
⌐	322	cobalt blue
⊥	336	navy
▽	356	light chestnut
s	407	grey chestnut
◺	434	light brown
∟	611	light olive brown
◇	801	dark brown
\	972	gold
◆	986	sap green

Techniques
* cross-stitch
* $^1/_4$ and $^3/_4$ cross-stitch
* backstitch
* overhand knots
* plaiting

Instructions

- Use two strands throughout design (unless otherwise stated), even for backstitch outlining.
- Backstitch ranch, horses, wagon, fence, tepees and fire with 986 sap green.
- Use 321 deep red to backstitch mouths on both bears.
- For the Cowboy's six buttons (4 x 972 gold on shirt and 2 x 310 black on vest), cross-stitch the single square, then outline the four sides to give definition. Same goes for the pads on the bears' paws in 310 black.

Finishing

- Outline the following items in 310 black.

  Cowboy: Hat, outer and inner ears, hatband, head, muzzle, eyes, nose, eyebrows, neckerchief, vest, shirt, all skin, pads of paws, holster and gun, belt and buckle, chaps, denim jeans, spurs and toes.

  Indian: All feathers on headdress, head, outer and inner ears, headband, head, muzzle, eyes, nose, eyebrows, teeth necklace, quiver plus arrows and strap, breastplate, all skin, armbands, knife handle and blade, loincloth, rawhide pants, bow and toes.

- For the string on the bow, sew a free (not attached except at each end) but taut length of 310 black to go behind his arm. I used four strands for extra strength.
- On the Indian's headdress, use 321 deep red to add feather tips to 46 of the feathers.
- For the six tassels on the Cowboy's chaps, I threaded my needle with equal length strands of 3 x 972 gold with 3 x 986 sap green and knotted twice before coming up from underneath the fabric at the designated dot. I tied two overhand knots exactly on the fabric, then cut the tassel to 1 cm ($^3/_8$").
- For the Cowboy's lasso, I threaded my needle with equal length strands of 6 x 321 deep red, 6 x 972 gold and 6 x 986 sap green and knotted them together. I brought the needle up from underneath the fabric at the designated dot on his paw, then pulled the needle off. I plaited these three colours, then formed three ovals with a tail (the end of the lasso which was the knotted end of the plait), then attached them to the cowboy's paw with small stitches. The lasso is to remain free-hanging to add movement to the design.

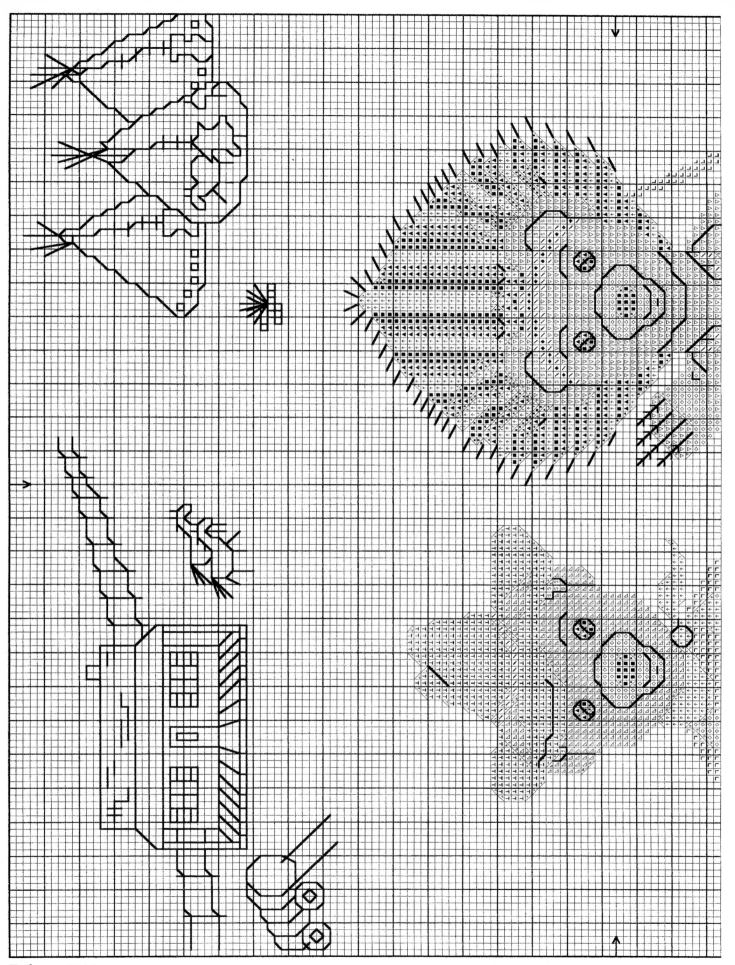

Enlarge 10%

Ⓐ

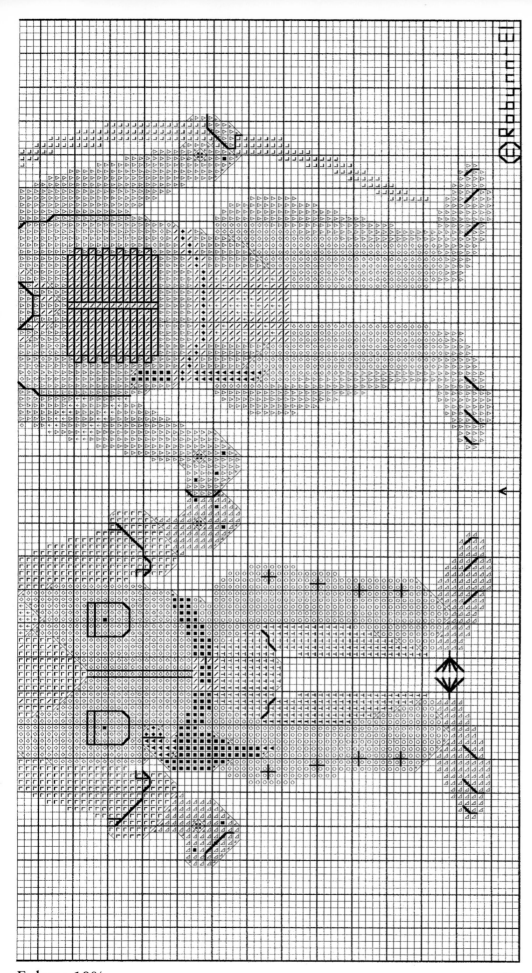

Enlarge 10%

Ⓑ

FAERY BEARS

WILD WEST BEARS

BLOOD BROTHERS

CLEOBEARTRA

RAPHBEARS

THE BEARTLES

BEAREO & JULIET

BEARZAN & JANE

SCARLETT O'BEARA

Super Bear and Vampire Bear
BLOOD BROTHERS

Robynn-E

BLOOD BROTHERS

**The finished design measures 20 cm wide
by 28 cm high (8" x 11").**

Fabric

A 30 cm by 45 cm (12" x 18") piece of smoky grey Aida
14 cloth (fabric pack size).

Threads

Symbol	DMC thread	Colour
▲	blanc	white
v	300	rich medium brown
∪	304	blood red
■	310	black
–	414	grey
△	550	rich purple
•	552	purple
s	603	girlie pink
＼	742	light orange
I	775	faded blue
>	796	royal blue
◇	801	dark brown
=	815	cherry red
⌐	996	light blue
◿	3776	light russet

Techniques

* cross-stitch
* $1/4$ and $3/4$ cross-stitch
* backstitch

Instructions

- Use two strands throughout design, even for backstitch outlining.
  Exception: for Vampire Bear, use three strands of white for the fur, to give density.
- There is no outlining on 'Blood Brothers'.
- Use 310 black to

backstitch Super Bear, Vampire Bear and the telephone box.
- Outlining for **Super Bear:**
  Costume, boots and cloak with 796 royal blue;
  'S' patch, belt and stripes on his boots with 742 light orange;
  'S' with the same 304 blood red;
  Arms, legs and head with 300 rich medium brown;
  Interior ear shape, eyebrows, nose, eyes, mouth, muzzle and paw pads with 310 black. He is looking a bit worried about Vampire Bear's proximity!!

- Outlining for **Vampire Bear:**
  Boot stripes, the 'V', checked vest, pink collar roll and upper line of the stripe on the base of his cloak with 603 girlie pink;
  Legs, arms, paw pads, head, ears, eyebrows, nose, eyes, muzzle, boots and purple cloak with 310 black;

The 'V' patch on his vest in the same 550 rich purple;
Backstitch his mouth with 304 blood red.
- Use 742 light orange to outline the cross on the coffin.
- Outline the telephone box details and windows with 310 black, as well as the coffin.

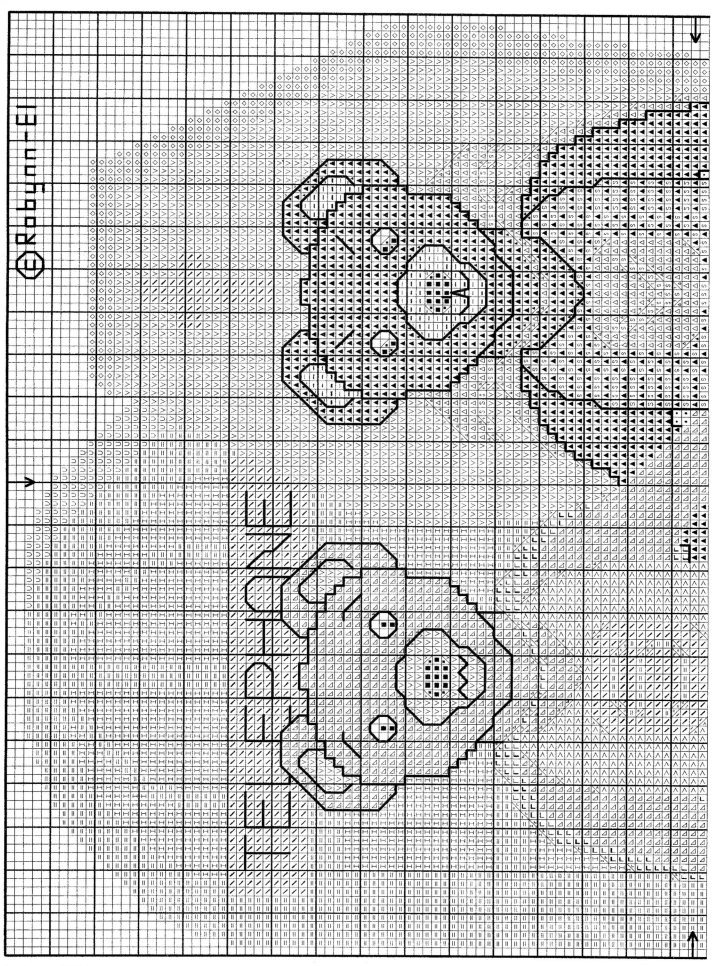

Enlarge 10%

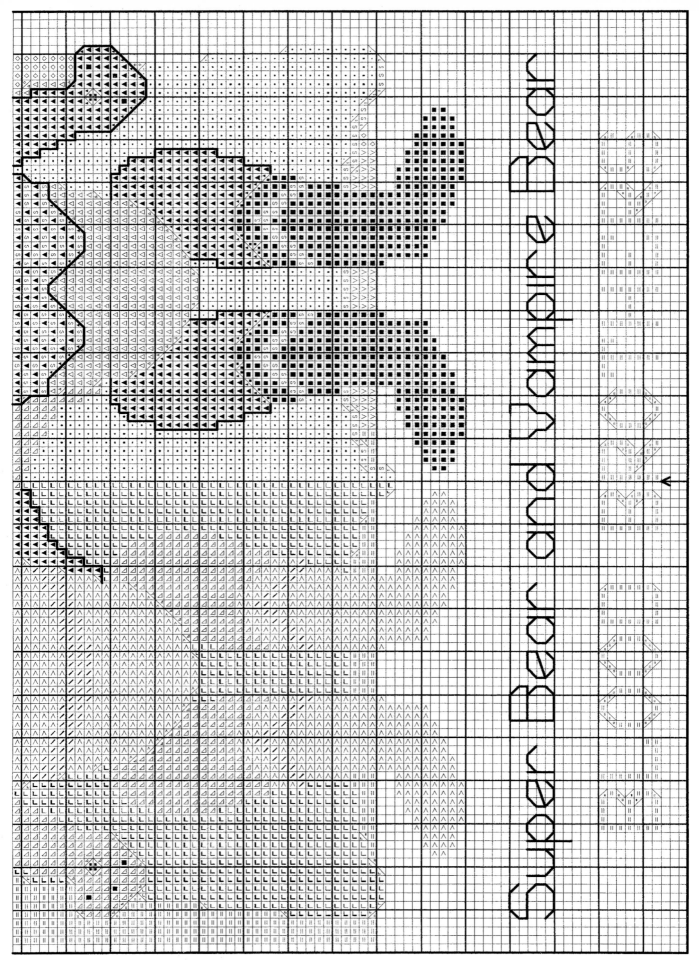

Enlarge 10%

Ⓑ

FAERY BEARS

WILD WEST BEARS

BLOOD BROTHERS

CLEOBEARTRA

RAPHBEARS

THE BEARTLES

BEAREO & JULIET

BEARZAN & JANE

SCARLETT O'BEARA

CLEOBEARTRA

The finished design measures 33 cm wide
by 26.5 cm high (13" x 10 $\frac{1}{2}$").

Fabric

A 30 cm by 45 cm (12" x 18") piece of cream Aida 14 cloth
(fabric pack size).

Threads

Symbol	DMC thread	Colour
▲	blanc	white
■	310	black
s	402	pale pumpkin
◸	552	purple
↓	553	light purple
•	600	crimson
▶	603	girlie pink
◇	632	landscape brown
\	742	light orange
>	820	midnight blue
≠	825	marine blue
□	906	grass green
◺	920	medium brown
∧	3781	Renaissance brown
△	3803	carmine
◆	3818	sap green
∨	3826	light clay
<	5282	metallic gold

To create Cleobeartra's see-through harem pants,

L bottom left to top right first stitch in 3826 followed by 3818 to complete the cross stitch.

= Bottom left to top right first stitch in 600 followed by 3818 to complete the cross stitch.

U Bottom left to top right first stitch in 3808 followed by 3818 to complete the cross stitch.

Techniques

* cross-stitch
* $1/4$ and $3/4$ cross-stitch
* backstitch
* straight stitch

Instructions

- Use two strands throughout the design, even for backstitch outlining.
- There is no outlining on the Egyptian hieroglyphics.
- For the palm fronds Cleobeartra's slave is waving, use 3818 sap green to backstitch the seven fronds and 906 grass green to indicate the separate leaves in straight stitch (backstitch over four squares).

- **Outlining the Slave:**
  Ears, mouth, nose, muzzle, eyes and pupils, eyebrows, face, hair, neck, arms, paws, chest, legs, feet and toes in 310 black;
  His 825 marine blue eye shadow in the same blue;
  Decorative collar and loincloth with 820 midnight blue.
- **Outlining Cleobeartra:**
  Ears, mouth, nose, muzzle, eyes and pupils, coloured eye shadows, eyebrows, face, hair, neck, arms, paws, outfit, legs, feet, toes, coronet, gold belt and bangles in 310 black.
  - Outline the couch, grapes and platter, golden chalice and palm branch in 310 black.
- The floor delineation ends in 920 medium brown backstitch.

Enlarge 10%

Ⓐ

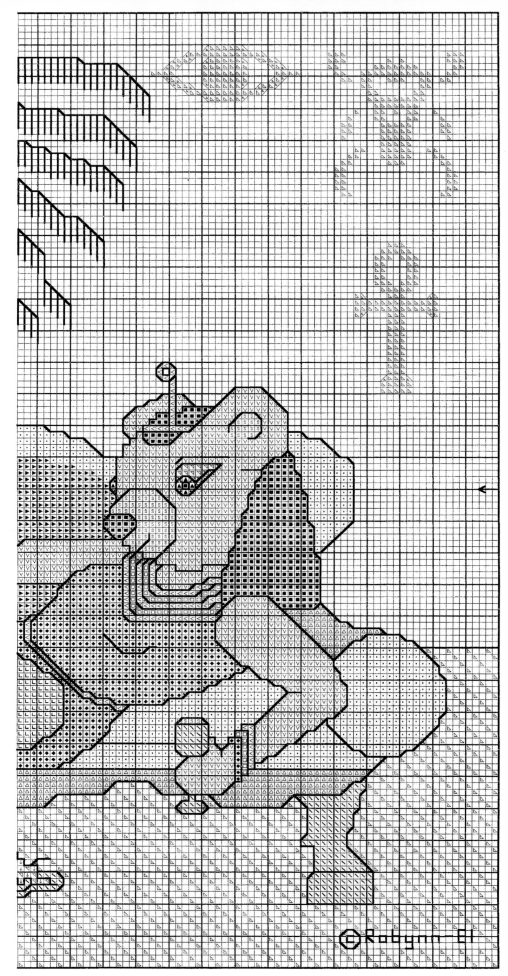

Enlarge 10%

B

RAPHBEARS

The finished design measures 22.5 cm high
by 36.5 cm wide (8 $\frac{3}{4}$" x 14 $\frac{1}{2}$").

Fabric
A 30 cm x 45 cm (12" x 18") piece of light blue Aida 14 cloth
(fabric pack size).

Threads

Symbol	DMC thread	Colour
▲	blanc	white
■	310	black
>	322	cobalt blue
∨	400	brick brown
I	402	pale pumpkin
H	699	forest green
◀	794	light blue
∧	797	deep denim blue
=	814	plum
L	833	pale olive
◇	898	mud brown
◆	911	dark ice green
◁	920	medium brown
∩	955	ice green
▽	956	musk stick pink
s	957	fairy floss pink
≠	3747	pale blue ice
T	3820	dark yellow sand
<	3822	flat yellow sand

Techniques

* cross-stitch
* $1/4$ and $3/4$ cross-stitch
* backstitch

Instructions

- Use two strands throughout the design, even for backstitch outlining.
- Complete the clouds before outlining the bear angels' wings and balustrade.
- Outline the stone balustrade and all bricks with 920 medium brown.
- Outline the larger bear's wings (on the left) and all the decorative patterns within those wings with 814 plum.
- Outline the smaller bear's wings (the bear on the right) and all the decorative patterns within those wings, with 699 forest green.
- Outline both bear angels with 310 black; their claws, body, muzzle, nose and all facial features including pupils.

Robynn-El

Enlarge 10%

Ⓐ

Enlarge 10%

B

THE BEARTLES

The finished design measures 35 cm across
by 24 cm high (14 $^3/_4$" x 9 $^1/_2$").

Fabric

A 30 cm x 45 cm (12" x 18") piece of pale rose pink Aida
14 cloth (fabric pack size).

Threads

Symbol	DMC thread	Colour
▲	blanc	white
U	221	red brown
s	223	pink satin
=	304	blood red
■	310	black
V	355	red chestnut
◺	356	light chestnut
◇	400	brick brown
▽	407	grey chestnut
–	413	dark grey
∟	436	whitewood brown
O	452	medium grey
◀	517	medium blue
≠	518	pale sapphire
/	647	chrome
T	725	mustard yellow
\	742	light orange
<	744	haystack yellow
→	745	pale yellow
I	746	off white
∩	783	mustard
⊥	820	midnight blue

Techniques

* cross-stitch
* $\frac{1}{4}$ and $\frac{3}{4}$ cross-stitch
* backstitch
* straight stitch (long tacking for the guitar strings)

Instructions

* Use two strands throughout the design, even for backstitch outlining (except for the guitar strings which must be worked with one thread only when you have completed the whole design.)
* There is no outlining on the floor or wall background pattern.
* Outline each white section of each guitar in the same colour as that particular guitar, e.g. blood red 304 outline of the white section on Paul's red guitar
* Use 310 black to outline guitar knobs, neck, guitar and black sections on each guitar, also the drum, drum platform, drum feet, cymbals, cymbal stands, Ringo's drumsticks, the side drum plus stand and 742 light orange tension rods.
* Backstitch 'The Beartles' in black when you have finished the whole large drum.
* Use black to outline everything on all four bears; hair, inner and outer ears, eyes, pupils, muzzle, nose, mouth, lips, neck, shirt, tie, lapels, buttons on Ringo and John's jackets, John's spectacles, jackets, cuffs, hands and finger delineation, groin, legs, feet and toes.

Enlarge 10%

Ⓐ

Enlarge 10%

BEAREO & JULIET

The finished design measures 37 cm high
by 23 cm (14.^{1}/$_2$" x 9")

Fabric

A 30 cm x 45 cm (12" x 18") piece of light grey Aida 14 cloth
(fabric pack size).

Threads

Symbol	DMC thread	Colour
▲	blanc	white
←	ecru	cream
■	310	black
s	353	peach pink
%	356	light chestnut
↑	407	grey chestnut
T	420	sandy brown
–	434	light brown
\	444	brilliant yellow
I	445	bright lemon
N	701	dark apple green
◆	722	pale orange
>	791	dark blue
∨	801	dark brown
U	815	cherry red
‖	890	jungle green
=	902	rich brown burgundy
△	915	deep pink
▽	918	rich brown
H	947	orange blaze
O	976	pumpkin brown
⌐	995	intense blue
◇	3031	dark chocolate
◸	3804	fuchsia

Techniques
* cross-stitch
* $1/4$ and $3/4$ cross-stitch
* backstitch
* overhand knots

Instructions
* Use two strands throughout the design, even for backstitch outlining.
* With 310 black, outline Juliet's cap, hair, face and features, arms, shoes, dress and sleeve flounces. For the architecture, outline the dark brown archway, both horizontal balustrades, each stone support and decorative rectangular blocks (two above and one below each support) and the dark brown stone floor (underneath supports) with black.
  Outline Beareo's ears, head, sword blade and handle in black.
* Outline the two single square gemstones on Beareo's sword handle with the same 444 brilliant yellow as well as his shoe buckles.
* Outline the 918 rich brown decorative features on the stone supports (small circle over the larger oval shape) with the same.
* There is no outline on either the brickwork or the trellis so it looks natural.

* Outline the 3804 fuchsia single flowers with the same, as well as the top of the double coloured flowers.
* Outline the bottom of the double coloured flowers with the bottom pink, 915 deep pink.
* Outline the leaves on the trellis with the same 890 jungle green.
* Outline Beareo's shoes, boots, orange tights, blue cloak, shirt, shirt sleeves and collar, yellow sleeve inserts and gloves with 791 dark blue.
* There is no outline around the light blue pattern on Beareo's collar or the orange decoration on the hem of his cloak.

Finishing
* Cut seven strands of thread, 9 cm (3 $1/2$") long without separating strands; four in brilliant yellow and three in 701 dark apple green. Knot each strand, then thread each through to the right side of the design, beginning with yellow (then alternate the colours) from the top of Juliet's cap on the straight left side. These will be left as free-flowing ribbons which can be ironed into place, left to hang or twisted artistically.

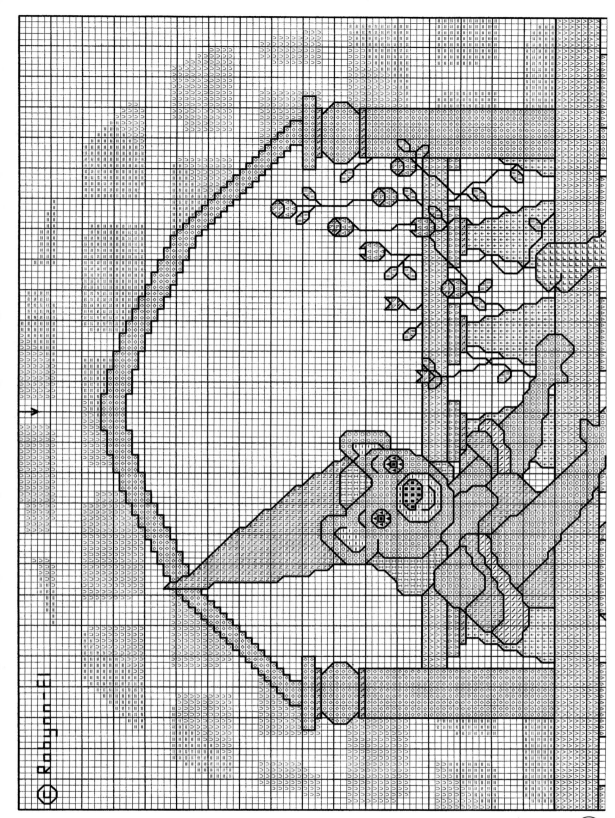

Enlarge 25%

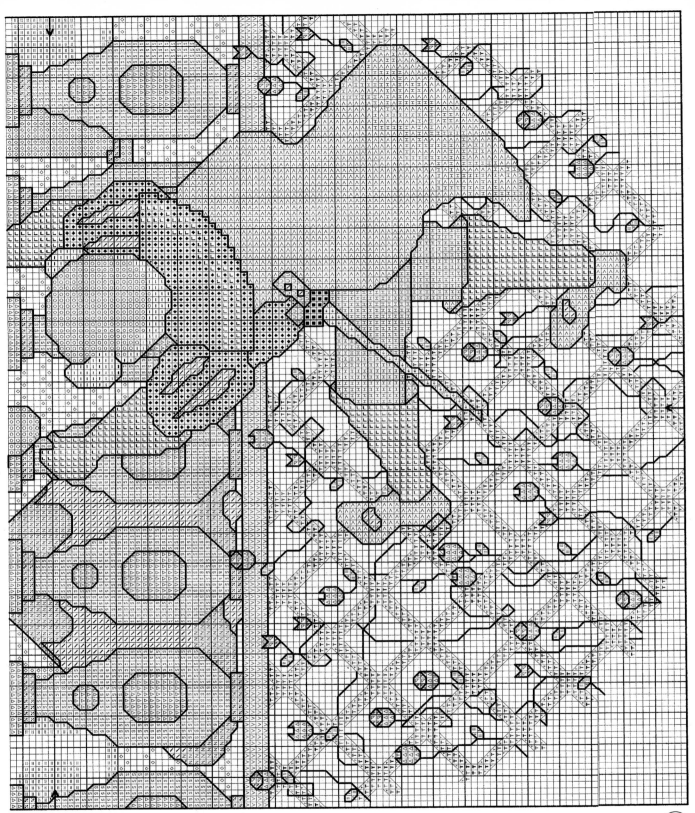

Enlarge 25%

Ⓑ

FAERY BEARS

WILD WEST BEARS

BLOOD BROTHERS

CLEOBEARTRA

RAPHBEARS

THE BEARTLES

BEAREO & JULIET

BEARZAN & JANE

SCARLETT O'BEARA

BEARZAN & JANE

The finished design measures 37 cm high
by 26 cm wide (14 $\frac{3}{4}$" x 10 $\frac{1}{4}$").

Fabric

A 30 cm by 45 cm (12" x 18") piece of textured-oatmeal Aida 14
cloth (fabric pack size).

Threads

Symbol	DMC thread	Colour
▲	blanc	white
∨	300	rich medium brown
■	310	black
I	422	fawn
◸	434	light brown
▽	600	crimson
□	703	light green
=	817	deep red
◇	838	mission brown
s	894	fairy floss
◆	905	bush green
H	910	mid apple green
⌐	943	jade green
↑	970	traffic orange
<	972	gold
I	991	vibrant grey green
←	992	medium jade
\	3827	iced pumpkin

Purchase 13 bugle beads for Jane's necklace; I used 5 red,
4 apple green and 4 yellow beads.

Techniques

* cross-stitch
* $^1/_4$ and $^3/_4$ cross-stitch
* backstitch

Instructions

- Use two strands throughout the design, even for backstitch outlining.
- When both bears are fully stitched, outline all their facial features, body parts, toes and claws, loin cloths and jaguar spots with 310 black.
- Outline the yellow and orange flowers plus their interior pistils with 817 deep red.
- Outline the fairy floss pink flowers and their pistils with 600 crimson.
- Outline all the long leaves with 991 vibrant grey green.
- Outline all the rounded monstera leaves with 910 mid apple green.
- Outline the vines with the same 838 mission brown.

Finishing

- With 910 mid apple green, backstitch Jane's necklace taking care to thread a red, yellow or green bugle bead (in that order) as you go, securing the bead simply by continuing to backstitch. Secure the end normally.

60

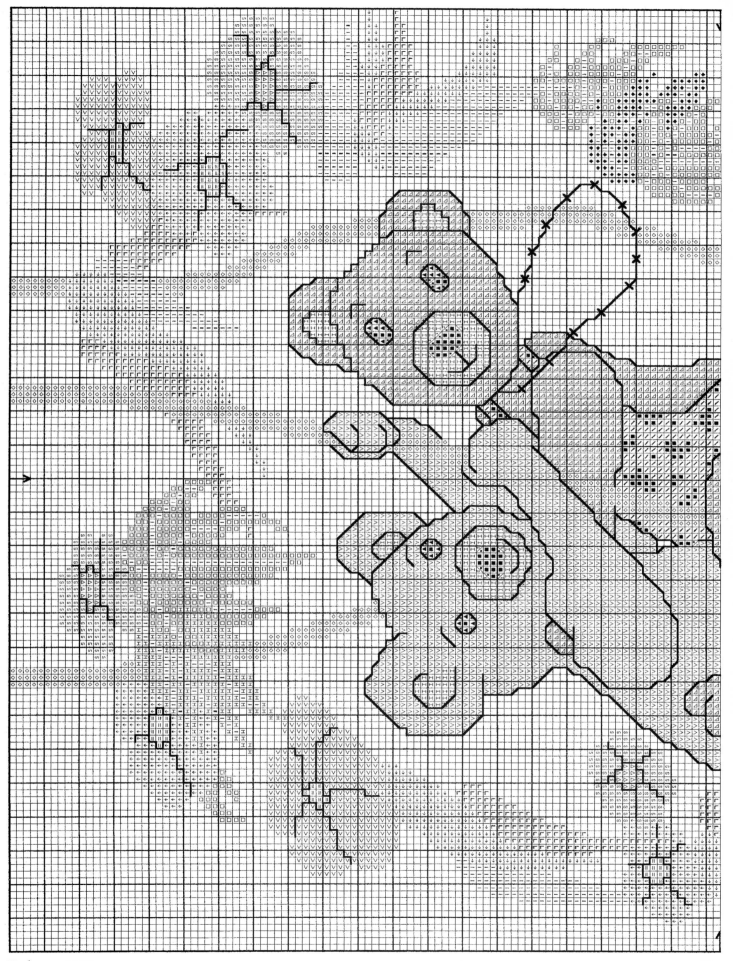

Enlarge 10%

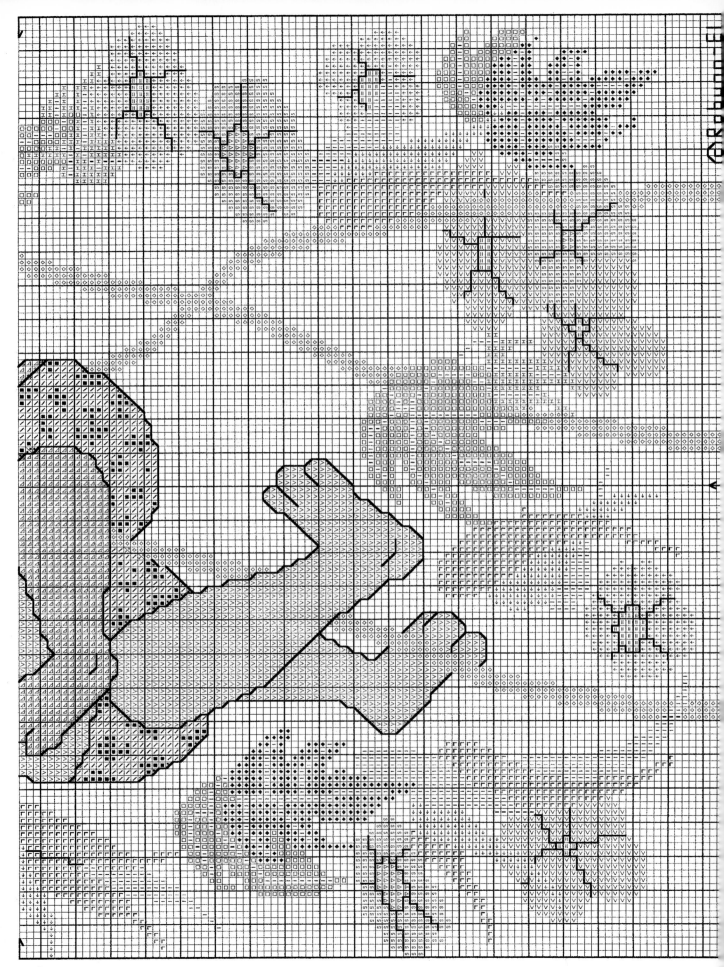

Enlarge 10%

SCARLETT O'BEARA

(or "Frankly Scarlett, I Don't Give a Darn!")

The finished design measures 35 cm high
by 24.5 cm (13 $^3/_4$" x 9 $^3/_4$ ")

Fabric

A 30 cm by 45 cm (12" x 18") piece of mauve Aida 14 cloth
(fabric pack size).

Threads

Symbol	DMC thread	Colour
▲	blanc	white
=	304	blood red
■	310	black
s	335	deep medium pink
–	413	dark grey
v	433	chestnut
△	550	rich purple
◇	898	mud brown
◆	943	jade green
←	959	light jade
◺	977	light pumpkin brown

Purchase 17 pink bugle beads for Scarlett's necklace and earring.

Techniques

* cross-stitch
* $\frac{1}{4}$ and $\frac{3}{4}$ cross-stitch
* backstitch

Instructions

- Use two strands throughout the design, even for backstitch outlining.
- Outline Rhett's sleeve with 413 grey then black so it shows up against the black jacket.
- Outline everything else on Rhett with black, including his trouser stripe, pupil and facial features. Backstitch his moustache twice.
- Outline Scarlett's skin, pupil and facial details, hair, bosom and finger details on glove with black; her white dress, fancy sleeve detail and gloves with 304 red; her waistband with 943 jade green.
- Outline the pink hearts with 304 red.
- For the flowers on Scarlett's dress, backstitch the petals with the same 304 red, then add backstitched leaves with 943 jade green.

Finishing

- Tack beads on one at a time where marked with a dot around her neck and one on her ear as an earring. Use normal sewing thread.

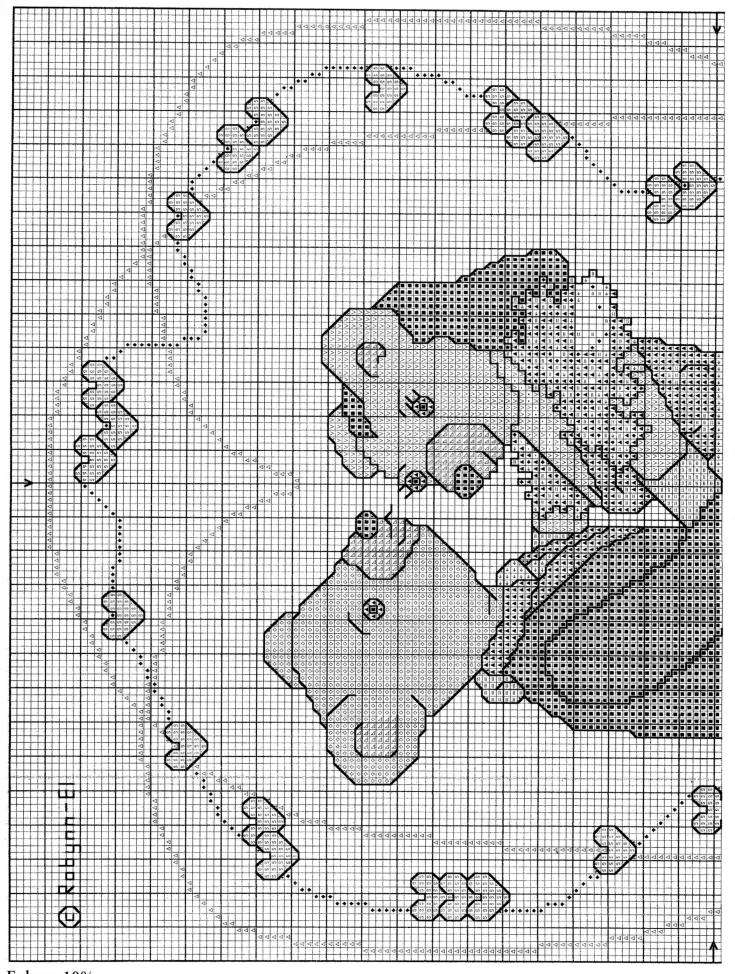

© Robynn-El

Enlarge 10%

Ⓐ

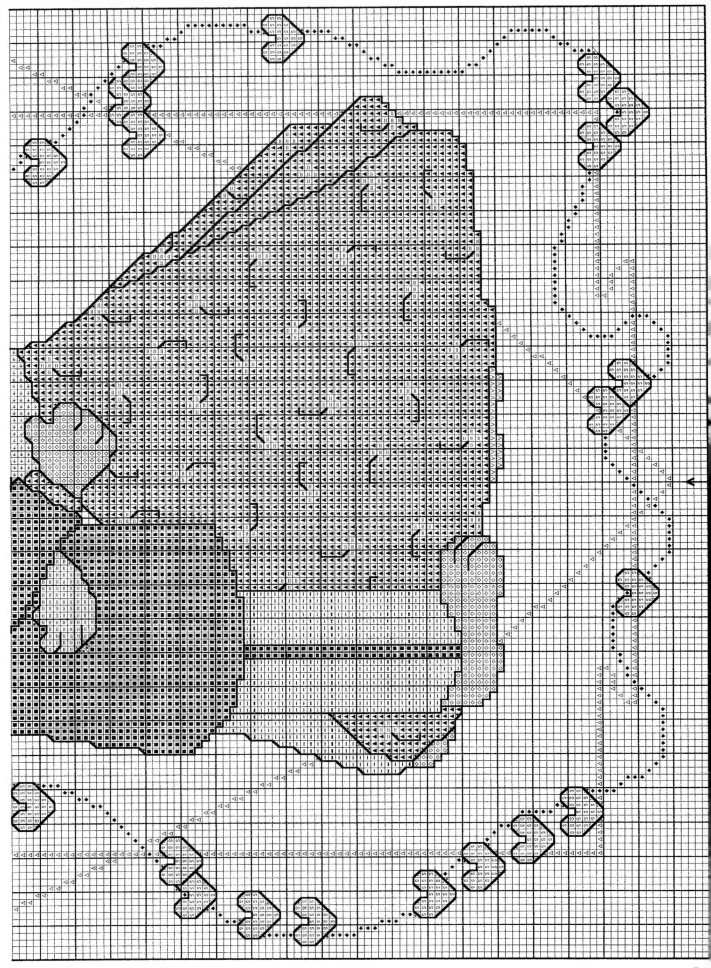

Enlarge 10%

Ⓑ